THE ROYAL WEDDING

A Creative Colouring Book
Unicolour Books

Printed by Createspace
Available from Amazon.com and other online outlets.

First Printing, 2018

ISBN: 978-1717339157

Prince Harry and
Meghan
Saturday 19th May

_____

TEST YOUR COLOURS

Made in the USA
Columbia, SC
05 May 2018